Oxblood

OXBLOOD

POEMS BY

Nicole Caruso Garcia

First published in 2022 by

Able Muse Press

www.ablemusepress.com

Library of Congress Cataloging-in-Publication Data

Names: Garcia, Nicole Caruso, 1972- author.
Title: Oxblood / poems by Nicole Caruso Garcia.
Description: San Jose, CA : Able Muse Press, 2022.
Identifiers: LCCN 2021060278 (print) | LCCN 2021060279 (ebook) | ISBN 9781773491059 (paperback) | ISBN 9781773491066 (ebook)
Subjects: LCGFT: Poetry.
Classification: LCC PS3607.A72198 O93 2022 (print) | LCC PS3607.A72198 (ebook) | DDC 811/.6--dc23/eng/20211213
LC record available at https://lccn.loc.gov/2021060278
LC ebook record available at https://lccn.loc.gov/2021060279

Printed in the United States of America

Cover image: *In Oilseed* by Gundula Vogel

Cover & book design by Alexander Pepple

Nicole Caruso Garcia photo (on page 79) by Studio392

Able Muse Press is an imprint of *Able Muse: A Review of Poetry, Prose & Art*—at www.ablemuse.com

Able Muse Press
467 Saratoga Avenue #602
San Jose, CA 95129

For Carlos, with love,

and in memory of Kim Bridgford

Contents

Meet me, Jesus, meet me.
Won't you meet me in the middle of the air.
And if these wings should fail me, Lord,
Won't you meet me with another pair. . . .

—Blind Willie Johnson
"In My Time of Dying" ("Jesus Make Up My Dying Bed")

Oxblood

Oxblood

Why will you take by force what you may obtain by love?
—From a 1609 speech by Chief Powhatan, as recorded by John Smith.

Go to Sheplers on North First in Tucson.
Buy yourself a pair of cowboy boots.

You're East Coast, so the salesclerk won't attempt
to sell you Tony Lama or Lucchese.

She'll steer you toward a discontinued pair
of Sanders, plain, just under ninety bucks.

And when you hesitate—*Cordovan?*—
she'll gently pull the wadding from their throats,

correcting you politely: *These are goatskin.*
Oxblood. Under other circumstances,

brown or black would do, but it's a long
walk back along a ledge of grief. These boots

must testify: a diamond ring is neither
branding iron nor fencing wire. Don't ask,

Why take by force what you can have by love?
Despite your Spartan fist, there's no redress.

So take the oxblood. Thank the lady for
her help, and yes, you'd like to wear them home.

For eight years wear them, staggered in between
your Goth phase, swing phase, punk, bohemian.

They'll frisk you at the Guns N' Roses show,
    so tuck a can of Mace inside the shaft.

When trouble parks his El Dorado just
    to follow you on foot, remember this:

each arch contains an eighteen-gauge steel shank.
    And when the mud-scabbed soles are wearing thin,

well, get them fixed. For twenty bucks they'll look
    as good as Lazarus. For eight more years,

wear them, in rain and snow and summer heat.
    Though late most afternoons the light forgives,

spills violet-blue, one day you must admit
    although the leather still looks plummy, half

the outsole stitching has dissolved like catgut,
    and the vamp is pulling free. Beyond

repair, yet beautiful with brokenness.
    Retire them beneath the guest room bed,

and in that kneeling, listen at the window
    to the swelling requiem of crickets.

If you have done all this, then stand. At first
    you'll feel no different. Yet, the sun will strike

within a copper sky, that barefoot hour
    when all your scorpions have turned to sand.

But suicides have a special language.
Like carpenters they want to know *which tools.*
They never ask *why build.*

—Anne Sexton
"Wanting to Die"

I

Appraisal

Once raped, you wear it daily, learn to see
the cut, the color, clarity, and carat.
Each time you try to square asymmetry,
it cleaves, reveals another jagged facet.

Fool, you think it fits inside one poem.
No, map with calipers and microscope
your story since you came to wear that stone:
flawed and heart shaped, bluer than the Hope.

Since you must wear it, hone it with precision.
Leave your wrists unslit, the blood unbled
to cut and polish sin to scintillation.
Woman, rise up from the rhinestone-dead.

Yet what can cut a diamond? Nothing can,
except the hardest substance known to man.

What Were You Wearing?

Because the body is a temple,
I wore the wakeful song of birds,
lay safe beside my lover, still.

Because the body is a temple,
when he trespassed like a vandal,
I had no robe but words.

Because the body is a temple,
I wore the wakeful song of birds.

Coloring Book of the Saints

Saint Francis of Assisi's tonsured head
was purple. My mistake. He seemed to wear
a beanie like the Pope's, so how was I
to know his head was partly shaved, a field
where God's light shone its holy tractor beam?
I felt uneasy, having wronged a saint.

The next page showed a young Italian girl.
Maria Goretti was not yet twelve,
but beautiful. Her story new to me,
it told of how, amid her household chores,
an older neighbor boy, enraged, had stabbed
her fourteen times "because she would not sin."

I tried to thumb its meaning like a bead
within a rosary, its place secure.
And on her deathbed she forgave the boy?
He had no halo, and he worried me,
as if I'd heard a jangling chain and feared
what dog might lurch into my yard or when.

I'd rather they had shown Bartholomew.
Beheaded, first he suffered skinned alive.
I could have taken comfort in such gore,
the barber-surgeon's knife in honest view.
Apostles were the renegades, grown men,
and yet Maria's wounds were on my page.

I searched cathedral rows of crayons, found
bright halo *yellow, red*, and *peach* for flesh.
Yet blunt with wear, they couldn't be precise.
I knew to hone one worthy I would have
to peel its sleeve, no measure too severe
when sharpening an instrument of God.

Dispatch

Unopened mail was still June-hot against
the cool Formica of the kitchen table.
I held his letter to the light, yet sensed,
if read, the words would be indelible.
I knew enough: they'd either scorn or praise.
I'd asked him not to write or call again,
for fear my love would smother my goodbyes.
How easy to elope with danger then.

So, where he'd tongued the V of envelope,
I replied, *REFUSED: RETURN TO SENDER.*
Outside, I squinted at the glinting tip
of noon, and though I let the letter swelter,
raised the mailbox flag so icy-gloved,
I mourned as I made ash of what I loved.

The Oldest Cruelty

A moment stuck in freeze-frame, rated R.
Your borders all redrawn—how small you are.

He liked Renoir, museums, yet beneath
the cheap veneer of culture lurked an ape.

He's golfing just as if it never happened.
For the course of womanhood it's par.

Who put what where, how many times and when.
His lawyers dig to undermine your rep.

You burn your fields, yet leaves curl inward like
Pompeiian lovers. Sulfur, ash to reap.

You hear it now, the rape joke frequency.
Antenna raw, you can't retune your ear.

How amplified, misogynistic lyrics—
catchy, though—in pop and rock and rap.

Cenozoic means *new animal.*
Not new. The oldest cruelty of this era.

Stack featherbeds and mattresses like flapjacks.
You feel it, like the princess and the pea.

No more, the gritty sweetness of his kiss.
He fit you like an Inquisition pear.

Your choicest parts hang spiraled in the trees
for birds to peck. There's nothing left to pare.

You search for *y* yet fall just short of prayer.

To the Undertaker

Undertaker, I have sought you;
hover close above.
My overtaker, faith-shaker,
was the man I loved.

Sew my useless jaw together;
drain my blood's scant volume.
He moved as though my lips were stitched
by all the days I'd loved him.

Your devotion lasts two hours.
Tend and wash my body.
In merely minutes he had made
unholy Holy Friday.

Fill me with your reeking fluid,
harsh, but not unkind.
Preserve my body with your proof;
his petrified my mind.

Pack my cavities with gauze;
make pretty perjury.
I thought I was a woman, loved;
I am an effigy.

Paint my face so lifelike they
will marvel at my charms.
"Who's that makeup for?" he asked.
Gawkers, now. And worms.

Oh, gentleman of more respect,
lay coins upon my eyes.
He made me lesser than a whore,
staked claim between my thighs.

I was his would-be wife, and still
you dress me for the church.
A gown of silken muslin for
a carcass with no worth.

Blood Villanelle

In a National Public Radio segment aired on January 25, 2013, titled "Impulsivity and Access to Means Drive Rising US Suicide Rate," an expert said that Britain reduced its suicide rate by no longer selling paracetamol (acetaminophen) in bottles where people could easily dispense and ingest all the pills at once, but rather in blister packs where the pills must be pushed out one at a time.

I wanted there to be a lot of blood,
although I'd dangled months resisting it,
as if I could forget the prick, the flood,

the only morning I'd said no. He'd slid
between my legs, and I dissolved to dirt.
Love's courtesy: he left no bruise, no blood.

And so began a courtship with the blade.
No pills or rope or freefall would anoint
me like the careful slash, hot prick, and flood.

Unmake as willfully as you would build.
We snowflakes are unique, like excrement.
I wanted there to be a lot of blood,

and, still as a Rosetta stone, be heard.
Don't brand me *coward, sick,* or *selfish*—not
unless you've felt the faithful prick, the flood,

the urgent call to close up like a bud,
yet split your ripeness open in a fit
of prayer, to drowse in petals of your blood,
and wake again, beyond the prick and flood.

When They Called My Name at Graduation

Perhaps you cast one final sidelong glance.
Across the lawn I drifted, a buoyancy
that everyone mistook for joy, despite
the chiseled smile of my figurehead,
the stirring of my black and aimless sails.

II

Auto-da-fé

Observe the bluish hue before the dawn,
when snowy trees play hide-and-seek, the grove
so halcyon and feathery with hush.

A twig lash scarcely blinks. As night's last flakes
fall soft as silent bells, a yawning moon
lays down her bobbin lace and fades to sleep.

When dawn turns violet, trees fringed in gowns
of icy arabesque then masquerade
and peek through veils like breathless woodland brides,

too rapt to know that they already wear
the color of surrender. Innocent
and cosseted as lambs, they stand condemned.

Lament the hour when one vermilion-robed
Inquisitor ascends and takes his seat
within the blue tribunal of the sky.

By noon, that wicked star will strip these maids
who blaspheme beauty too ethereal.
He'll let wet lace drip down their length and pool

around their feet. They'll stir the wind with cries
of *Miserere mei, Deus*, stretch
their limbs toward heaven, shivering with fire
till mourning doves all startle from their hands.

Dear Reader

> *Is not the most erotic portion of the body where the garment gapes? . . . the intermittence of skin flashing between two articles of clothing . . . between two edges . . . it is this flash itself which seduces.*
>
> —*Roland Barthes,* The Pleasure of the Text

You come to hear me come undone, the diction
taut, then loose, from my chameleon tongue.
You sometimes wonder if it's fact, the friction
of my lover's stubble where I'm stung.
You gape at what the gaping might expose.
What will my inky fingerprints betray?
I lie sincerely. My words conceal, disclose
no more, no less, than paint or bronze or clay.

Yet what I thought was simply ink grows thick
and hardens, forged like opalescent stone
or bee-flecked amber, set in a mosaic
I can't stop. In truth, I'm not just shown
in dishabille. However crude or sacred,
soon all I've offered God, to you, lies naked.

The Raft

Each breath a splinter, how I dreamt of land.
Below the spooling stars, a man cried out.
My fever grasped at echoes for his hand.
To my companion I became devout
and wound around him like a tourniquet.
My legs were threads of jute; half hitches moored
him, though the sea had thrashed his silhouette.
And over time, some wounds the salt air cured.
Naïve, I thought that we would find true north,
two separate wrecks more tethered by each kiss.
But winds unstitched my oath, and drifting forth,
I let him sink beneath the green abyss;
for what I'd clung to while delirious
was never love, but something gangrenous.

Counterfeiter

Inside a diary quite pink and tame,
in purple ink my first love's name was set.
But I was nine, so names renounced became
confetti I could scatter and forget.
Compelled to purge each scrap of evidence,
I ripped. The rabbit on the cover smiled,
more willing to be marred by this offense
than by these false devotions be defiled.

I grew, pronounced my love upon men's lips
in earnest. Feathery, each stroke I signed,
my body scrawled across the mattress. Script,
so deftly forged, leaves volumes to unbind.
And now, mind stained with my calligraphy,
what can I tear with schoolgirl luxury?

La femme obscure

Though sailors woo her, flashing galleons
and cannon bronze,

let phalanxes of stars retreat. She needs
no glinting guards.

She is both empress and the castle keep,
her fortress deep,

five thousand fathoms of obsidian.
Dismiss the moon

drawn like a scimitar against the throat
of creeping light,

for she is sanctuary strong as stone,
her court within

great vaulting halls of coral tapestries,
her diary's

smooth decades strung like pearls around her wrist.
With merely mist

for battlements, she stands, a citadel
defended well.

At daybreak she emerges molten gold,
both coy and bold,

behind her ear an orchid of white foam.
Beneath that bloom,

her naked shallows freckled warm with light,
she blinks, and yet

her stoic stare belies each wound or kiss
in her abyss.

She cradles good men whom she could not save,
attends each grave,

yet wrestles scoundrels to her chamber floors.
Despite the boors

who offer bagatelles of bristly lace,
cast emptiness

and jetsam in her depths like an ersatz
trousseau, their nets

she silvers bright with fish. And with each wave,
she tries to heave

ashore the contents of her deepest trench,
as if the beach

could bear inscription carved like rare white jade.
Across mute sand

she hears the wind bring ballads laced with rum
and myth's perfume.

Ships' amber lanterns make men's shadows grow
with claims to know

her countless coves, her vast domains;
yet she remains

aloof and sprawling nude from sky to shore,
la femme obscure.

Route 15: Daydream

As I pump my gas along the highway,
        cars that tunnel out of winter sun

zip by like match strikes, reignite the cold.
        I wonder what these folks are hurtling toward

or from. But none look happy at that speed,
        as if their breathless joy could not keep up.

Yet when I turn away, sun's sudden touch
        behind my knees revives me, makes me wonder

where he is. Perhaps a conference room?—
        speaking in a deep, oak business tone

to those who'll never hear his ape impression?
        Though the gas is eighty bucks, I smile,

because tonight I'll make him sloppy joes,
        the kitchen incandescent with our voices.

This wind, it isn't always like a jack-
        knife to the heart. If motorists could slow

to watch the locomotion of my breath,
        they'd see his name float out from underneath

my hood, a puffy parka so bright red
        he teases, calls me *Gumdrop.* I don't mind.

Today the sky burns blue with alchemy,
        but they just rocket past as I secure

the gas cap, as I shift my weight on frozen
        rosy tiptoes like some hot-coal hopscotch,

wishing that the folks who've found true love
        would smile or wave or horn-blast hallelujah.

III

Harvest Moon

When or if or soon, will we be? Aloof, yet
like a chrome oasis, your white-hot neon
"O" says, *Though the heavens are dark and silent,*
come, I am OPEN.

See my face aglow with your glowing. Are you
out of reach? You borrow and pinball sunbeams;
I am bells bells bells at your touchless touch, through
miles of midnight.

Let me taste you, golden-white apple, swollen
in the night's cool basin. Like saints, we linger
brow to brow within a confessional of
trees. Won't you tell me?

I could grasp a blemish of stars like scattered
jacks, yet were I able to coax you down from
orbit, I would not give you back. Your tranquil
sea and this fever.

I Never Fell in Love with You

To fall in love implies a lack of choice,
as if I were cartoonish, maladroit—
and love, an open manhole to avoid.

To fall suggests a kind of loftiness,
that I began in some exalted place
and not the aerie of my loneliness.

To fall like rain, or tears, or mercury,
a pawn of Cupid or of gravity.
No. With my grappling hook, I climbed precisely.

To fall—*kerplunk*—is stumbling, imperfection.
No, I would brave the hot tar of rejection
to wear the ermine cloak of your affection.

I built a trebuchet and aimed to sail
beyond your moat, over your castle wall.
I launched, I soared in love; I did not fall.

Ode to Carlos

Your eyes are like the Thames at noon, midspring:
soft gray-green sprigs of velvet moss and sage.
I do, I do, the river seems to sing.

My eyes are brown and ordinary things,
and yet you call them *doe eyes* and your refuge.
Your eyes are like the Thames at noon, midspring.

You are the muse to rouse ink's uttering;
yet who can love in ink upon a page?
I do, I do, the river seems to sing.

We've crossed the Tiber, Arno, walked along
the Seine and Manzanares; yet, each voyage,
your eyes are like the Thames at noon, midspring.

And if I were to lose my wedding ring,
I'd make a vow each sunrise; that is marriage.
I do, I do, the river seems to sing.

When you have gone, I'll keep imagining
that if I were to make a pilgrimage
to see your eyes again, at noon, midspring,
Adieu, adieu, the river still would sing.

Embrace

Against
tuxedoed night
I stand at the window
and in the champagne of moonlight
undress

Barren

Only
a five-pound sack
of flour in her arms
as children sled and laugh beyond
bare trees

Another Rorschach

Once more, these monthly inkblots swaddled in the trash:
the prayers that rows of votives snicker into ash,
no help for hunger, just a mockingberry stain,
a crimson phone booth from which failure calls again.

Once more, the kiln door of the cosmos, slamming shut,
the smear of rouge that pales the cheek and turns the gut,
defeat's dark wine, decanted by a nemesis,
a ruby crown demoting queen to baroness.

The still-warm stamp of exile in carnelian wax,
famed scarlet signature that sells a blank tableau,
luck's thousand paper cranes unfolding like a hoax,
the dregs on porcelain where tea leaves answer: *No*.

Once more, a cheap carnation's brown-edged sympathy,
a neon retina fluorescing *VACANCY*.

Haiku

flourishing—
bloodgood maples we named
instead of children

If You Are Reading This

If you are reading this, my love, then we
have reached "for poorer" since our wedding day.
Forgive this frugal anniversary;
unwrap these fragments, gifts I tucked away:

I gather birdsong, chirps that percolate,
the scent of dew and diesel in the air.
Although the sun unlocks the morning gate,
the moon still lingers, just to say she's there.

The bookstore beckons addicts to her ink.
I fan through brand new titles, crisp and sweet,
inhale the tomes until so paper-drunk
the clerk ejects me back out on the street.

And then, a quest for subtler liquors brings
me to a dozen dog-eared stacks to search.
I hold their scent of reverence in my lungs
like incense burning in an ancient church.

At home, I find transcendence in the act
of making lunch. Behold this afternoon,
a jar of peanut butter, whorl intact,
a landscape yet uncharted by a spoon.

And soon, above the hammock where I sway,
the clouds are powdered wigs with woolly curls.
While edged in pink and cream, against a day
so blue, a vision of Versailles unfurls.

By night, our yard is filled with lullabies,
when thriftiness has shut off every lamp,
and silent music of the fireflies
plucks darkness softly as a golden harp.

And all these things I gathered just for you,
in case we were too poor for fine hotels
or jewels or furs or villas with a view.
Reserve the satin sheets for jezebels.
Just cool, clean sheets against our sunburned skin,
sheets tucked so tight we have to wiggle in.

Snow White's Plea to the Huntsman

Asleep, I shiver in a silken gown
and wait for you to find me in the dark.
Don't let me waken shackled to a crown,
too drowsy to resist that royal mark.
You saved me once and fooled the wicked queen
who craved a lung-and-liver fricassee.
Yet served a hoax, she licked her fingers clean.
By sparing me your sword, you captured me.
Let moonlight vigil lead you to my lips
and prove your kiss will break this spell's embrace.
The prickly arrows of your cheek eclipse
affection from the smoothest princely face.
Such knaves can plunder castles, trinkets, art;
but only you can breach my fortressed heart.

IV

Capacity

I sometimes wonder if I'm just a ghost:
when I'm alone, unbuttoning a cuff.
When daubing perfume on each perfect wrist.

When folding garments, each a hollow self.
A *suicide*: an entry on an intake
form, a footnote to a headstone, stiff

and imprecise, an ill-fitting sack.
I run my lips across my wrists (kiss, kiss)
for proof I live. And if they're not a trick,

a mockery, then I must confess
the love and decades I might not have had.
I tremble for a truer name for this,

this having risen from the never dead.
I am whole, yet hyperventilate—
I am a *could-have-cut*, a *would-have-bled*.

I've housed the breath before you consummate
the *carpe mortem*, glittering with intent.
Resolve that sober can intoxicate.

Prostrate, I'd given angels my consent.
I'd chosen my finest dress, a lacy sheath,
as if to bandage sin in sacrament.

We label mostly in the aftermath.
We can't quite throat a word that could contain
the moment that the apple felt Eve's breath.

Some membrane torn already in my brain,
what hand had held me here against my will?
An object set in motion stays in motion.

The only word for that is *miracle*.
That, too, becomes a thing that you survive.
It changes you, the knowledge you would kill—

to occupy the hour at such an octave,
prayer so pure you'd call it blasphemous.
What simple word could show you where I live?

The whole transcends the parts I name with ease.
(The knife was aptly named: *utility*.)
I need a word to hold all this because

I did not fail; my name means *victory*.
And there's a word for what he did to me.

Annual Giving

Don't ask me for an annual donation
when I fought daily for my resurrection.
What would he have to do to face expulsion?

Would he have had to violate your daughter?
Would he have had to desecrate your altar?
I dropped the class we'd planned to take together.

You had a reputation to protect.
Rape is a prickly word; thus, the verdict:
Responsible for Sexual Misconduct.

You levied sanctions—flimsy, every one—
mere inconvenience. Hampering his fun.
He didn't break a rule; he broke a person.

To live off campus senior year? No loss.
Kicked off the golf team, no more captain status.
Banned from buildings where he had no classes.

To see his Judas face kept trauma fresh:
his force the day they nailed our Savior's flesh.
And now you call me up and ask for cash.

What shepherd says, *Oh, injured lamb, be healed:*
the wolf is just a dog. He's not expelled—
we'll keep him to one corner of the field.

Was it because I hadn't told my parents,
and his—despite their lack of affluence—
hired lawyers? Asked to verify the contents

of a file compiled by those strangers,
I saw there, held by wire fasteners,
a punctured stack of all my love letters.

What insult, that instead of *social justice*
your therapist put crayons in my fist.
Well, color me an insurrectionist.

I'd hoped. Yet at the time, it had to be
enough to know Authority believed me.
I carried on my studies quietly.

I kept high grades while lying in my grave.
My shroud I tore to poems, each a votive
wick. Oh, oily rag. Oh, Molotov.

Don't ask for giving when you pardoned taking.
Don't sell me snake-oil justice for my aching.
A punishment needs teeth, and then it's speaking.

To what now could my money testify?
You found him guilty, yet you just stood by.
We threw our caps into the same blue sky.

Ghost Ship

At a distance, candles guttering
can look like party lights. The way a ghost ship
might seem from shore.

It may have seemed I was carousing. It may
have hurt you seeing my illuminated
decks, my painted flags livened by wind.

Despair is so immaculate a plague.
A healthy vessel still will float, although
you pillaged all the spirit from its hold.

A ship like that may run aground or wreck
against the cliffs.

Adrift between the quick and the dead,
it is not sorry, does not love or hate—
it lists.

Stop saying *Brave,*

so brave, you're very brave—
as if you hadn't heard my words at all.
There is no summary, no whole, just parts.
They'd taken everything that had been sworn.

I'd loved him in betrothal till betrayal.
I chose adjudication, not a trial,
so I wouldn't have to see him face-to-face.
So I wouldn't have to face a crowd.

And yet, to find him guilty of one rape
required I confess to countless deeds.
That's true, but out of context. Yes and *Yes.*
Vivisection means while you're still living.

Raised to look a person in the eye
when spoken to or speaking, I answered the
adjudicator's questions, saw the searchlights
of his eyes were pale and not unkind.

He paused to ask, *Is it too cold in here?*
When I said no, he asked if I was sure.
It's just that you keep closing up your jacket—
tightly—like you're absolutely freezing.

I looked down and saw myself contorted:
knees crossed, arms crossed, each fist a clutch of fabric.
His office windowless and small, he said,
Your body language, it's . . .

I came forward, true, but only when
five months had passed, and someone asked me if
I wanted to report it. I said, *I guess.*
I couldn't muster *Yes.*

Stop saying *Brave*.

There is no tidy summary, just parts:
love letters weaponized, eyes pale
and not unkind, the jacket and the buckling,
his question, *Are you cold?*

Gossamer

She greets me with a happy shriek, my pseudo-
stalker: former student, porcelain faced,
a clown doll smiling so as not to shatter.
I notice she has dyed her blonde hair red,
a shade to match the latest teenage queen,
her polka-dotted Wellingtons so big
they swallow her up to the knees. A wall
of windows separates us from the rain.

We discuss her latest piece of writing.
Despite the new red 'do, despite her clothes
as bright as gumballs, she's so gossamer
I see her demons, like the day she giggled,
If I said that I got raped, would you laugh?
She's memorized dull details of my life,
as if to look for clues to figure out
just how to wrestle demons to the ground.

I want to say, *You're doing it all wrong.*
You think, in time, that demons pack for exile?
Your story is tattooed along your bones,
unspeakable, a host of roiling dragons.
Embrace the creatures coiled around your limbs.
Get up each day and neatly fold your shroud.
Make every sinew bold, declare yourself,
and clench the bright blue dragon of your fist.

But there's no graceful way to teach these things.
By dinner she'll be back in New York City,
ascending subway stairs, a manuscript
beneath her vellum skin. I'd like to think
although she's flanked by demons, they recede
in darkness as she surfaces, aloft.
Yet there's no fierceness rising out of ash,
just her red hair fanned against the skyline.

Blues Triolet

Such pretty grit is in the ashes,
what flecks could resurrect despair?
Like track-tossed bottles sunlight smashes,
such pretty grit is in the ashes.
Through the train car window, flashes
of graffiti flame like prayer.
Such pretty grit is in the ashes,
what flecks could resurrect despair?

In Praise of Gray

My graying hair, for now, is free of dye.
There's darkness plenty in my alibi,
no rage against the youth-obsessed. (I'm vain.)

    I've reached the age my mother was had she been
    roused from sleep to go identify
    my body, had I bled it. In sterile light,
    she would have clutched my father as they cried,
    their firstborn's hair forever chestnut brown.

My graying hair—
hurrah!— it grows more wiry and defiant,
a crown to celebrate and testify
I'm here. And though I never can atone
for the crush of dawn they'd nearly known,
just look: the sunlight can't deny
my graying hair.

V

Stigmata

He raped
me Holy
Friday &
I grieved
as if he'd
died that
milk-sky
morning
& filthy I felt my spirit split from bottom to top
not the clean temple veil God split from top to bottom
every sighting of a cross drew fists of salt on raw
red loss:
my love
my Self
my God
& yet my
heart is a
revival in
the desert
its cross
remains
barbaric
crucifix
whether
in wood
or sterling
or gold leaf

Extension

This assault, was it of a sexual nature? . . . These things happen. I suggest you throw yourself into your work.
—Dr. ________, Professor of Art History (1993)

It was ~~kind advice.~~
cruel.

I sat in ~~the front row and earned A's.~~
a chair in his office and cried.

It was ~~September, and my topic was due soon. The paper wasn't due until December.~~
too late. I'd asked too much.

It was nakedness—~~the prostration of asking—that made my eyes well up, calling for explanation.~~
over which he flung his coarse response.

These things happen~~? "To *whom*? Not anyone *I* know," I wanted to say.~~
as close as love.

The professor knew ~~much about Michelangelo's *Pieta*.~~
no pity; this was Modern Art.

I was trying ~~to throw myself into my work; I'd planned ahead.~~
not to throw myself from the marble window ledge of my dorm room.

I had been handed the ~~Modern Art Syllabus.~~
Rape Syllabus.

Slide #1: ~~Gustav Klimt's *The Kiss.*~~

A crucifixion.

Slide #2: ~~Salvador Dali's clock-melt, *The Persistence of Memory.*~~

A crucifixion.

Slide #3: ~~A leather Mies van der Rohe chair.~~

A crucifixion.

The professor offered his advice coolly~~, like water ladled into a beggar's cup~~.

It tasted like a drink from Duchamp's *Fountain*.

If the professor ~~wouldn't grant an extension for me, Little Miss Honor Society, then for whom?~~

wasn't calling me a liar, *These things happen* meant *You aren't rare or special.*

He was~~, by November, reading my introduction aloud to the class as an exemplar.~~

making an example out of me.

How close I was ~~to calling home to say, *Come get me*~~.

I didn't want to drop out.

~~He failed me.~~

I earned an A. He failed me.

He wrote me ~~off.~~

a glowing letter of recommendation.

~~I threw myself into my work.~~

I threw myself into my work.

Three Landays

Are you pacified? Where is your wrath
that our daughters are born with rape whistles in their mouths?

* * *

Mother, my poems may upset you,
though I do my best to shape neat squares from exit wounds.

* * *

Some words I seek—not for narrative—
but as one claims a body, flesh over which to grieve.

Burden Blues

I thought my burden was bespoke couture:
a lace yoke made-to-measure, haute couture.
Then I saw ten like it at the Goodwill store.

A packhorse saddle-bagged, the burden cruel.
The nuggets must be gold!—a mite less cruel.
Turns out they're iron pyrite; I'm the mule.

No common crown of thorns could this queen bear.
Yet now I grasp the cap and bells I bear:
I've been an April fool twelve months a year.

Warning Sign

He threw me over his shoulder in a caveman's carry,
his townhouse full of partygoers. I struggled: *Put me down!*
Did they think it was a game? My hair grazed the ground.
One shoe threatened to fall. Were they daunted by his golfer's build?
He hauled me up two flights—basement to bedroom—right
past Catholics with high SATs. Once he freed me, I'd see

him hurl the photo album at the wall. Was I okay? No one came to see.
That tantrum, months before the wound I'd ultimately carry,
started when his buddies razzed him. I pleaded, *They took it right*
out of my hands! I forgot that photo was even in there. I retreated down
the basement steps, but it only made the ugly in his eyes build.
He would not be laughed at, not on his own stomping ground.

When he ordered me upstairs, I stood my ground:
You can't make me. But to help the crowd unsee
that photo of him in a mask of my red satin panties—lest it build
a reputation—I had to be sacrificed. Now I'm too volatile to carry.
Hypervigilant, some might say. Yet if I let my guard down,
chance may dredge up my mortified face—even when men do right:

when I see a firefighter bearing a survivor on his shoulders, I'm right
back on that staircase. The newsfeed rips the ground
from under me. Vowing to never again be upside down,
I too often cast myself as Wonder Woman. My first landlady I still see
flicking her cigarette: *Frank ever put his hands on me, they'd carry*
him out in a pine box. Love a gentle man, and wager he won't build

a gallows, your footing at his pleasure. No matter the life I build—
degrees, publications, travels, a love who treats me right—
I was that upended woman. Mentioning a black belt, a permit to carry,
I make some prick at a luncheon uneasy, so he probes for background:
Geez, what happened to you? He squints to see
which wire to cut, the blue or the red. But *Calm down*

is just another way of saying *Bow down.*
Of saying *I'm afraid what an angry woman will burn or build.*
Of saying *Look at you on that staircase.* The whole party can see
up my skirt, bystanders knocking back beers while Mr. Divine-Right-
of-Kings carts me off like spoils of war, ass six feet off the ground.
I became, although at one time heaved into that caveman's carry,

a woman who began spitting fire and rock into the sky in downright
anger, not knowing it would build for her solid ground,
that with each hiss of lava entering the sea, her voice might carry.

Have You Ever Been a Victim of Violence? Eleven Reasons Why I Don't Check *Yes*

For Dr. Leslie Goldstone-Orly

I

Because the box, once X'd, can't be undone.

II

Because to check the box is like a sadder
version of *I VOTED*.

III

Because I'll disappoint my angel of
a gynecologist. She'll ask me, *When?*
and see I've kept the truth from her for years.

IV

Because—damn it—I resent the box,
just waiting there to ambush me again.

V

Because I bristle at the label *victim*.
And *survivor*. Can't win. Both dice are loaded.

VI

Because the waiting room is Starbucks-busy.

VII

Because the box is no confessional.

VIII

Because there is no exorcist on staff.

IX

Because don't ask me to concede a thing
when it's already such a feet-in-stirrups-
flashlight-on-my-cervix kind of day.

X

Because of women wearing crowns of thorns
far thornier than mine.

XI

Because what grit I've got I ration.

Philomela's Starfish Tongue

you forced
yourself
beyond
my lips

sliced out
my tongue
so what?
know this

my tongue
will not
relent

these hands
not made
to weave

a tongue
beyond
lament

a tongue
not made
to grieve

sliced off
this sea-
star limb
defies

regrows
more tongues
resounds
war cries

brute Tereus
your muscle spent
so primitive
ineloquent

your weapon: flesh
your weapon: steel
your weapons few
I shall prevail

barbarian of Thrace
you are no king to me
Athenian, I'm formed
from this deformity

Athenian, I am
a chariot of war
gilt wheels of starfish tongues
each spoke a carnivore

one tongue has flowered myriad spears
so strike until you dull your sword
I've feasted on the crust of tears
don't look for mercy from the gods

The Pope's Vagina

After Sharon Olds's "The Pope's Penis"

It relaxes beneath her cassock, muscular
walls of a sovereign city-state.
It has unknotted the last beads of cardinal blood.
A grotto in a patch of dandelion white,
a hooded figure oversees its almond-shaped gate,
a pink cowrie shell retaining
the tang of Eden.

At the Field's Edge

I knelt & dug

was there another choice? / I had to
clear these stones these land
mines if / I hoped
to get across

no sharper pace / if I hoped
to ever plant one good
green thing

VI

What the Angel Saw

My earthly cousin often had received
him at her gate, a man of twenty, sworn
in their engagement. Likewise young, her warm
limbs tendered toward his hands, the only man
that she had ever sheltered there. Yet when
she woke on Holy Friday, knowing that
it was Your day of suffering, her voice
still velvety with sleep, she told him no.
I hovered there, forbidden to uproot
the twisted will of man, and saw him rape
her, Lord, with gentle violence, as if
he could possess the world of her, as if
her worth began and ended in that grove.

He soon dismounted so indifferently
she thought her protests made him change his mind.
She turned, her back a wall dammed up against
a ghost of trust. Her nakedness was marked
by neither scratch nor bruise, and yet I saw
the brambles tear her soul-flesh as she seeped
with knowledge that he had not stopped on her
account, but only after he had filled
her with his insult. Lord, I held her and
with unguent traced the constellations of
her wounds. She lay there garlanded in grief,
tongue dumb to speak the curdling word, yet said,
It doesn't mean you have the right. He claimed,

If I am not entitled, then who is?
She curved toward window light, faint though it was,
and like a sunflower she hung her head.
I said, *Fear not, you are a child of God,*
though she lay stillborn in my arms. She hushed,
as if no nails had pierced her through, yet by
those wounds You drew her closer, proof she found
unbearable and yet miraculous.
She prayed: *How dare I ask the crucified*
for help? . . . Still I believe in You and pull
the sheet around my ribs, as if I could
conceal the truth and not offend Your eyes . . .
and yet, I need for You to see me, God.

The third day came. She sang in Easter Mass
and pinched her hand with crescents. Lord, I saw
the weeks she stayed, her fury when his priest
declared it was not rape. Yet still she kept
her vow, one night unhinged her knees in full
forgiveness. Yet, when she recalled the times
that he had palmed her belly, naming their
imaginary children, then she knew
that she must bury love, must lay no child
within the splintered cradle of his arms.
As summer idled, she said please and thank
you, smiled for photographs, yet every cross
renewed her Golgotha, from steeples to

the scarecrows crucified in fields. That fall,
she seeks distraction at a party, fades
within a crowd. He does not see her. When
she sees him laugh as though no sacred thing
were ever lost, she hastens home, resolved
to bleed herself as white as apple flesh.
I chase her disappearing breath, and though
she sinks to hush her lips against the floor,
her voice transcends the dead bolt of despair.
Convulsed with keening, primal prayer, she rakes
the carpet, begs, *Send angels.* Cries drown out
the neighbors' timid knocks where they begin
to gather at the threshold. Lord, her mind

delights to cut red ribbons at her wrists,
to harvest grief and have me lay her at
Your feet. The blade at rest within her desk
is startling comfort, often palmed and clicked
out quarter inch by quarter inch. She writes
no note, abandons words as impotent
apostles. Bless her suffering, that one
day she might voice her testament. She strains
to rise and gather into her best dress,
yet here I root her to the floor and clothe
her in a gift of armor. Lord, restore
the orchard of her heart, a warrior
whose blossoming begins with her defeat.

Acknowledgments

My grateful acknowledgments go to the editors of the following publications where these poems, some in earlier versions, first appeared:

Able Muse: "Burden Blues"

Antiphon: "Capacity," "Ode to Carlos"

Crab Orchard Review: "Annual Giving," "The Pope's Vagina"

Italian Americana: "*Have You Ever Been a Victim of Violence?* Eleven Reasons Why I Don't Check *Yes*"

Measure: "The Oldest Cruelty," "Philomela's Starfish Tongue"

Mezzo Cammin: "Another Rorschach," "Appraisal," "*Auto-da-fé*," "Barren," "Blues Triolet," "Coloring Book of the Saints," "Counterfeiter," "Extension," "Harvest Moon," "*La femme obscure*," "Oxblood," "Route 15: Daydream," "Snow White's Plea to the Huntsman," "Three Landays," "To the Undertaker," "Stop saying *Brave*," "What the Angel Saw"

Modern Haiku: "Haiku [flourishing—]"

ONE ART: a journal of poetry: "At the Field's Edge," "Ghost Ship," "In Praise of Gray," "*What Were You Wearing?*" "When They Called My Name at Graduation"

The Orchards Poetry Journal: "Dear Reader" (a variation originally appeared in the *Ledge* as "Tiles of the Mosaic"), "Embrace"

PANK: "Stigmata"

Poetry Midwest: "The Raft"

The Raintown Review: "Blood Villanelle"

Rattle: "Warning Sign"

The Rotary Dial: "I Never Fell in Love with You"

Willow Review: "Dispatch," "Gossamer," "If You Are Reading This"

My gratitude to the fine people at Trumbull High School, with especially heartfelt thanks to the English Department for their encouragement during my tenure there, and for their continued enthusiasm and support.

Thank you to the writing communities that have fostered my growth and where I have encountered such kindness, especially Eratosphere, the Poetry by the Sea Conference, and the West Chester University Poetry Conference. Deep appreciation for the friends, editors, and fellow poets in these spaces and beyond, who have offered invaluable encouragement, support, friendship, or inspiration, including Ned Balbo, Melissa Balmain, Meredith Bergmann, Maryann Corbett, Mark Danowsky (aka "The Arctic Fox"), Jehanne Dubrow, Pete Duval, Rhina P. Espaillat, Anna M. Evans, Annie Finch, Daniel Galef, Russell Goings, Tim Green, Katie Hoerth, Jeff Holt, Beth Houston, Charlotte Innes, Allison Joseph, Siham Karami, Karen Kelsay, David M. Katz, Jean L. Kreiling, Matt W. Miller, Marilyn Nelson, Alexandra Oliver, A. E. Stallings, Linda Stern, Maria Terrone, and the late and dearly missed: Susan de Sola and Jon Tribble.

My gratitude to the curators of reading series for their invitations to share and hone these poems with audiences: Harvey Soss at Artful Dodgers Poetry; Kate Bernadette Benedict, Wendy Sloan, and Anton Yakovlev at Carmine Street Metrics; Chris Belden and Katherine Schneider at FUMFA Poets and Writers Live.

Warm thanks to family and friends for their kindhearted support and enthusiasm, especially Lisa Acerbo, Nicole Azze, Emma Balter, Andrea Bertone, Holly Cashman, Ellen Demotses, Jodi Netting-Festa, Carlos Garcia, Sr., Christine Garcia, Kathryn Graham, Kim Ratliff Hall, Christine Heeg, Carol-Anne Hicks, Stephanie Jalowiec, Kristen Kravecs, David Palmer, Linda Paslov, Kerstin Rao, Anne Rizza, Becky Rodia Schoenfeld, Karlen Shupp, Irene Sommers, Jessica Spillane, and Kristen Veenema Stryker.

I am deeply thankful for the enduring friendship of Jason Azze, my very *first* first reader.

Big love to the women who saw this moment for me when it was still hidden to myself: Jackie Hennessey and Hope Spalla, who celebrated with joy and kept pointing toward the horizon. Profound thanks for your steadfast belief, loyal heart of friendship, backbone of support. Words can't express what it meant to me along the way—and means to me now.

Blessings to my Connecticut Writing Project writing group, whose critical insight, honesty, and deadlines helped me bring the manuscript for this book to fruition. Seven years of friendship and laughter—may it continue! I cherish you all—Bob Darken, Bill McCarthy, Jack Powers, Julie Roneson, Del Shortliffe, and Darcy Pennoyer Smith—and I marvel at your talent. I owe a debt of gratitude to Bob for the invitation that changed my life.

I also would like to extend warm thanks my editor and publisher at Able Muse Press, Alexander Pepple, for believing in my work and helping bring this book to life. Thank you for all you do for poetry. My gratitude to Mark Jarman for selecting *Oxblood* as a finalist for the Able Muse Book Award.

I am grateful to my parents Georgiana and Louis Caruso, and to my sister Denise, for their faith, love, and support.

This collection is offered in memory of, and with heartfelt gratitude to my teacher, Kim Bridgford, whose example, graciousness, guidance, longstanding support of my work, and friendship blessed me in immeasurable ways. Words are inadequate to say what her presence in my life meant.

Finally, to Carlos—my beloved husband, compass, and constant. You are the finest man I know, and I am deeply thankful for our life together. Love always.

Nicole Caruso Garcia is an American poet and educator. Born in New Jersey, she was raised there and in Connecticut where she now resides. Educated at Fairfield University, she holds a BA in English and Religious Studies. After seven years in the corporate sector, she earned her MS in Education from the University of Bridgeport and taught English at Trumbull High School for fifteen years. Garcia serves as associate poetry editor at *Able Muse* and as an executive board member at Poetry by the Sea, an annual poetry conference. Her work appears in journals such as *Atticus Review, Crab Orchard Review, DIAGRAM, Measure, Mezzo Cammin, Modern Haiku, ONE ART: a journal of poetry,* the *Orchards, PANK, Plume*, the *Raintown Review, Rattle, RHINO, Sonora Review, Spillway, Tupelo Quarterly*, and the anthologies *Extreme Sonnets* and *Extreme Formal Poems*. Garcia's manuscript for *Oxblood* was named a finalist for the Able Muse Book Award and the Richard Wilbur Award, and a semifinalist for the Anthony Hecht Poetry Prize and the Philip Levine Prize for Poetry. Her work has received the Willow Review Award, won a 2021 Best New Poets honor, and has been nominated for the Pushcart Prize and Best of the Net. Visit her at www.nicolecarusogarcia.com.

Also from Able Muse Press

Jacob M. Appel, *The Cynic in Extremis: Poems*

William Baer, *Times Square and Other Stories; New Jersey Noir: A Novel; New Jersey Noir (Cape May): A Novel; New Jersey Noir (Barnegat Light): A Novel*

Lee Harlin Bahan, *A Year of Mourning (Petrarch): Translation*

Melissa Balmain, *Walking in on People (Able Muse Book Award for Poetry)*

Ben Berman, *Strange Borderlands: Poems; Figuring in the Figure: Poems*

David Berman, *Progressions of the Mind: Poems*

Lorna Knowles Blake, *Green Hill (Able Muse Book Award for Poetry)*

Michael Cantor, *Life in the Second Circle: Poems*

Catherine Chandler, *Lines of Flight: Poems*

William Conelly, *Uncontested Grounds: Poems*

Maryann Corbett, *Credo for the Checkout Line in Winter: Poems; Street View: Poems; In Code: Poems*

Will Cordeiro, *Trap Street (Able Muse Book Award for Poetry)*

Brian Culhane, *Remembering Lethe: Poems*

John Philip Drury, *Sea Level Rising: Poems*

Rhina P. Espaillat, *And After All: Poems*

Anna M. Evans, *Under Dark Waters: Surviving the* Titanic*: Poems*

Stephen Gibson, *Frida Kahlo in Fort Lauderdale: Poems*

D. R. Goodman, *Greed: A Confession: Poems*

Carrie Green, *Studies of Familiar Birds: Poems*

Margaret Ann Griffiths, *Grasshopper: The Poetry of M A Griffiths*

Janis Harrington, *How to Cut a Woman in Half: Poems*

Katie Hartsock, *Bed of Impatiens: Poems*

Elise Hempel, *Second Rain: Poems*

Jan D. Hodge, *Taking Shape: Carmina figurata; The Bard & Scheherazade Keep Company: Poems*

Ellen Kaufman, *House Music: Poems; Double-Parked, with Tosca: Poems*

Len Krisak, *Say What You Will (Able Muse Book Award for Poetry)*

Emily Leithauser, *The Borrowed World (Able Muse Book Award for Poetry)*

Hailey Leithauser, *Saint Worm: Poems*

Carol Light, *Heaven from Steam: Poems*

Kate Light, *Character Shoes: Poems*

April Lindner, *This Bed Our Bodies Shaped: Poems*

Martin McGovern, *Bad Fame: Poems*

Jeredith Merrin, *Cup: Poems*

Richard Moore, *Selected Poems;*
The Rule That Liberates: An Expanded Edition: Selected Essays

Richard Newman, *All the Wasted Beauty of the World: Poems*

Alfred Nicol, *Animal Psalms: Poems*

Deirdre O'Connor, *The Cupped Field (Able Muse Book Award for Poetry)*

Frank Osen, *Virtue, Big as Sin (Able Muse Book Award for Poetry)*

Alexander Pepple (Editor), *Able Muse Anthology;*
Able Muse: A Review of Poetry, Prose & Art (semiannual, winter 2010 on)

James Pollock, *Sailing to Babylon: Poems*

Aaron Poochigian, *The Cosmic Purr: Poems; Manhattanite (Able Muse Book Award for Poetry)*

Tatiana Forero Puerta, *Cleaning the Ghost Room: Poems*

Jennifer Reeser, *Indigenous: Poems; Strong Feather: Poems*

John Ridland, *Sir Gawain and the Green Knight (Anonymous): Translation;*
Pearl (Anonymous): Translation

Stephen Scaer, *Pumpkin Chucking: Poems*

Hollis Seamon, *Corporeality: Stories*

Ed Shacklee, *The Blind Loon: A Bestiary*

Carrie Shipers, *Cause for Concern (Able Muse Book Award for Poetry)*

Matthew Buckley Smith, *Dirge for an Imaginary World (Able Muse Book Award for Poetry)*

Susan de Sola, *Frozen Charlotte: Poems*

Barbara Ellen Sorensen, *Compositions of the Dead Playing Flutes: Poems*

Rebecca Starks, *Time Is Always Now: Poems; Fetch, Muse: Poems*

Sally Thomas, *Motherland: Poems*

Paulette Demers Turco (Editor), *The Powow River Poets Anthology II*

Rosemerry Wahtola Trommer, *Naked for Tea: Poems*

Wendy Videlock, *Wise to the West: Poems; Slingshots and Love Plums: Poems;*
The Dark Gnu and Other Poems; Nevertheless: Poems

Richard Wakefield, *A Vertical Mile: Poems; Terminal Park: Poems*

Gail White, *Asperity Street: Poems*

Chelsea Woodard, *Vellum: Poems*

Rob Wright, *Last Wishes: Poems*

CPSIA information can be obtained
at www.ICGtesting.com
Printed in the USA
JSHW020221110622
26906JS00005B/203